Seven Words for Three Hours

Also edited or co-authored by Edmund Newell

SEVEN WORDS FOR THE 21ST CENTURY

THE WORLDS WE LIVE IN
(with Claire Foster)

WHAT CAN ONE PERSON DO?
(with Sabina Alkire)

Seven Words for Three Hours

*A Good Friday Meditation
in Words and Music*

Edited by
Edmund Newell

Music by
Adrian Snell

DARTON·LONGMAN + TODD

First published in 2005 by
Darton, Longman and Todd Ltd
1 Spencer Court
140–142 Wandsworth High Street
London SW18 4JJ

ISBN 0 232 52645 1

A catalogue record for this book is available from the British Library.

The last seven words are best known in traditional language. For this reason all references
to them are from the Revised Standard Version. All other biblical references and quota-
tions are taken from the New Revised Standard Version.

Designed and produced by Sandie Boccacci
Phototypeset in 12/15.5pt Minion
Printed and bound in Great Britain by
The Cromwell Press, Trowbridge, Wiltshire

For Susan and Dave

Contents

Part One: The Context

Lent Course 2012

The Seven Last Words of Christ
RICHARD HARRIES

①

The cross in the 21st century
ROWAN WILLIAMS

Part Two: Seven Words for Three Hours: A Good Friday Meditation in Words and Music

At the sixth hour

'Father, forgive them; for they know not what they do' (Luke 23:34)
EDMUND NEWELL

②

8   Contents

List of contributors

Words

Sabina Alkire is an economist, Research Associate at the Global Equity Initiative, Harvard University, and a non-stipendiary priest at St Stephen's, South End, Boston MA.

Giles Fraser is Team Rector of Putney and Lecturer in Philosophy at Wadham College, Oxford.

Richard Harries is Bishop of Oxford.

Edmund Newell is Canon Chancellor of St Paul's Cathedral and Director of the St Paul's Institute.

Tarjei Park is Vicar of Golders Green.

Rowan Williams is Archbishop of Canterbury.

Lucy Winkett is Canon Precentor of St Paul's Cathedral.

Music

Adrian Snell's career as a composer, songwriter, performer, recording artist and music therapist spans thirty years. He has performed world-wide, with many TV and radio appearances to his credit. His latest CD, *The Cry: A Requiem for the Lost Child*, was recorded with the choir of Winchester Cathedral.

Hannah Alkire is a classically trained cellist who is equally at home performing with symphony orchestras and rock groups. She and husband Joe Scott form the duo Acoustic Eidolon, which performs extensively throughout the United States and beyond, and whose broadcasts for PAX Television have received national awards in the USA. She has made solo appearances at St Paul's Cathedral and Westminster Abbey.

Joe Scott studied guitar at the Guitar Institute, Hollywood, and was co-founder of the group Wind Machine, before joining Hannah Alkire to form Acoustic Eidolon.

CD track list and credits

1. At the sixth hour ('The World is Full of Tears')
2. 'Father, forgive them; for they know not what they do' ('Kaddish for Bergen-Belsen')
3. 'Truly I say to you, today you will be with me in Paradise' ('Burdens of Guilt')
4. 'Woman, behold your son! ... Behold, your mother!' ('Behold Your Son, Behold Your Mother')
5. *'Eli, Eli, lama sabachthani?* ... My God, my God, why hast thou forsaken me?' ('Credo')
6. 'I thirst' ('They Shall be Comforted')
7. 'It is finished' ('Golgotha')
8. 'Father, into thy hands I commit my spirit!'('The Surrender')

All music composed by Adrian Snell, with additional contributions by Hannah Alkire and Joe Scott.
Adrian Snell: piano, vocals.
Hannah Alkire: cello.
Joe Scott: guitars, guitar synths.

The CD was recorded at Coupe Studios, Boulder, Colorado, by John McVey. Additional recording and mixing at Absolute Sound Recording, Berthoud, Colorado, by Joe Scott. Mastered at Airshow Mastering, Boulder, Colorado.

Creative Development: Edmund Newell and Adrian Snell.
Music published by Serious Music UK Ltd.
Adrian Snell: www.adrian-snell.com
Hannah Alkire and Joe Scott: www.acousticeidolon.com

For information about events related to this book and CD visit www.seven-words.org

Preface

In 2002, Darton, Longman and Todd published the book and CD *Seven Words for the 21st Century*. Based on the traditional format of using Christ's 'Seven Last Words from the Cross' for devotional meditation, the book's contributors reflected on how Christ's words spoke to them, and to society at large, at the start of the twenty-first century. Adrian Snell responded to the contributors' reflections with his own contemporary musical interpretations.

Since its publication, it has been pleasing to discover that *Seven Words* has been well received across the spectrum of church denominations and traditions, and by those concerned with Christian–Jewish relations. *Seven Words* has also been used as the basis for study groups and Good Friday services as well as for personal study and meditation.

On Good Friday 2003, the Three Hours' Devotion at St Paul's Cathedral, London, was based upon *Seven Words,* and involved several of the contributors. Soon after, the organisers of the service were asked by a newly formed organisation in the United States, Episcopalians for Global Reconciliation (EGR), whether it would be possible to adapt *Seven Words* and use it to help launch the organisation. EGR was established following the events of 11 September 2001. Its purpose is to foster spiritual renewal within the Episcopal Church by encouraging church members to engage with and respond to global poverty and inequity, particularly by supporting the Millennium Development Goals.

And so, in Lent 2004, a revised version of *Seven Words,* focused on EGR's aims and objectives, went 'on tour' in the USA with services at Trinity Church, Boston, St John the Divine Cathedral, New York, and the National Cathedral, Washington DC.

Seven Words for Three Hours is not so much a second or revised edition of the original book and CD, but a reworking of some of the earlier material and the inclusion of much that is new, for a different purpose and a wider audience. It is based on the material used in the services in the USA, and retains a strong Christian–Jewish dimension for reasons that will become apparent in the first address. This new version is designed to be easier to use for Lenten study than its predecessor, and in particular it is intended as a ready–made 'Three Hours' Devotion' resource for Good Friday.

Seven Words for Three Hours is in two sections. The first section reproduces chapters by Richard Harries and Rowan Williams that appeared in the original version of *Seven Words*. Many people have commented on how useful Richard Harries' overview has been to understand the development of the Good Friday liturgy and the history of the use of the Seven Last Words of Christ in music. This chapter provided some of the background material for a BBC Radio 4 programme *The Seven Last Words* broadcast in Eastertide 2005. The chapter by Rowan Williams, 'The cross in the 21st century', is a profound statement on the meaning of the cross in contemporary Christian thinking and provides the theological context for the rest of the book.

The second section of the book and the CD provide the materials for a Good Friday Three Hours' Devotion. The texts and music can be used as they are for public worship, or adapted if required. Together, they are designed to take under three hours to deliver, leaving ample time for silent prayer, reflection and congregational singing. The text is part address and part meditation; the more meditative parts are in italics. If reading aloud, the pace and tone should be varied accordingly. As long as the music is played in public for the purpose of worship it will not infringe any performing rights laws. Alternatively, the written reflections and CD could be used by individuals for private meditation on Good Friday, again over three hours, or dipped into during Lent or Passiontide for shorter period periods of study and reflection.

As with the original *Seven Words*, this version could also be used for Lent study groups. However, the reflections are considerably shorter than in the original version, making it easier for participants to prepare for discussion, or to read the reflections at the beginning of the discussion. At the end of any discussion group we would recommend a time for prayer and silent reflection, and to end by listening to the appropriate track on the CD, using a cross or crucifix as a visual focus.

I am extremely grateful to all who have contributed to this project. For the texts, I thank Richard Harries, Rowan Williams, Giles Fraser and Tarjei Park for their original work which we have used again, sometimes adapted, and Sabina Alkire and Lucy Winkett for new and reworked contributions. On the musical side, Adrian Snell has responded to the new or revised reflections with great skill and enthusiasm with a powerful new recording. This has provided the opportunity for Adrian to work more closely and creatively with the cellist Hannah Alkire, and with the guitarist Joe Scott. We are extremely grateful to the staff of Coupe Studios, Boulder, Colorado, where most of the CD was recorded, in particular to our engineer John McVey. The CD was produced by Joe Scott, who also did additional recording and production at his own studio, Absolute Sound Recording, for which we are extremely grateful. Susan Newell has been a companion and support to all involved in this project, and indeed has contributed to it in many ways. It has also been a delight to work on this project with Virginia Hearn and Elizabeth Piercey at Darton, Longman and Todd.

EDMUND NEWELL
St Paul's Cathedral, September 2005

Part One
The Context

The Seven Last Words of Christ

RICHARD HARRIES

Towards the end of the fourth century a pilgrim by the name of Egeria or Etheria, thought to be a Spanish nun, visited the Holy Land. An astute observer, Egeria recorded in a travelogue details of the many sites she visited, people she met and acts of Christian worship she attended. Included in her *Travels* is an account of a devotional service held in Jerusalem on the Friday of the 'Great Week', the day known to us now as Good Friday. She mentions that during the service the 'holy Wood of the Cross' was on display and venerated (and kept under the protection of the bishop and deacons because someone once bit off a piece and ran away with it!). She then describes that for three hours from noon – the hours that Christ is believed to have hung on the cross – there was a service of readings on the theme of Christ's passion, interspersed with prayers and hymns. Egeria's account is the first reference to a devotional service of this kind.[1]

Sixteen hundred years later, the Three Hours' Devotion is the most popular of the Good Friday services. It is often based on a series of meditations on the 'seven last words' – those phrases recorded in the gospels as being uttered by Christ as he hung on the cross:

> 'Father, forgive them; for they know not what they do.' (Luke 23:34)

'Truly, I say to you, today you will be with me in Paradise.'
(Luke 23:43)
'Woman, behold, your son! … Behold, your mother!' (John
19:26f)
'Eli, Eli, lama sabachthani? … My God, my God, why hast
thou forsaken me?' (Matt. 27:46)
'I thirst.' (John 19:28)
'It is finished.' (John 19:30)
'Father, into thy hands I commit my spirit!' (Luke 23:46)

The three hours from noon lend themselves to a period of prayer and
reflection, as the worshipper symbolically joins Mary, John and the
other followers of Jesus waiting at the foot of the cross. The seven last
words provide a helpful structure for this, drawing the worshipper
into Christ's suffering and the tumultuous events of Good Friday.

The seven last words have long been used as a set of passages for
reflecting on Christ's passion. The earliest collective reference to the
seven last words occurs in an eighth-century prayer of the Venerable
Bede, which contrasts them with the seven deadly sins. However, it was
probably not until the late seventeenth century that they came to be
used in the context of a devotional service. The introduction of such a
service is attributed to a Peruvian Jesuit priest, Fr Alonso Messia
Bedoya, in Lima sometime after 1687. Whether or not Messia's service
was original is uncertain, as there is a reference to something similar
conducted by a Franciscan priest in the earlier part of the century.
Nevertheless, it was Messia's version that was published and became
widely adopted in Latin America and Europe.

A significant moment in the history of the seven last words was the
introduction of Messia's service into the devotions of a group of pious
Catholics in Cadiz, Spain, sometime in the 1760s. This group, known
as the Fraternity of the Ancient Mother, met regularly to meditate on
Christ's passion in a cave under the Chapel of the Rosary, known as
Santa Cueva (Holy Cave). The Fraternity came under the spiritual
direction of a wealthy priest, Don Pedro Saenz de Santa Maria, who

introduced Messia's service and had a grand oratory built on Santa Cueva. The significance of this is that in the 1780s the composer Joseph Haydn was commissioned to write a piece of music based on the seven last words for use in Cadiz. It is speculated that this was in connection with the blessing of the Santa Cueva oratory in 1783, although this does not tally with Haydn's own account of events. In 1801 he wrote:

> It was about fifteen years ago, that I was asked by one of the Canons of Cadiz to compose a piece of instrumental music on the Seven Words of Jesus on the Cross. At that time it was the custom every year during Lent to perform an Oratorio in the Cathedral at Cadiz, the effect of which was greatly heightened by the *mise-en-scène*.
>
> The walls, windows and pillars of the church were draped in black cloth, and the religious gloom was lightened by one large lamp hanging in the centre. At mid-day all the doors were closed, and the music commenced. After a fitting prelude, the Bishop ascended the pulpit, recited one of the Seven Words, and gave a meditation on it. When it was ended, he came down from the pulpit and knelt before the altar. The interlude was filled with music. The Bishop mounted and left the pulpit for a second time, a third time, and so on, and on each occasion, after the close of the address, the orchestra recommenced playing.[2]

Whether or not there is a direct link between Haydn's *Seven Last Words* and Santa Cueva, what is significant is the introduction to Cadiz of the service based on the seven last words, as it led to the commissioning of the music by Haydn. Haydn's *Seven Last Words* quickly became one of his most popular works – with the original orchestral version later scored for both string quartet and quintet, which allowed it to be performed more easily and more widely, as well as for choir.

One interesting feature of Haydn's composition is that after the seventh word there is a final adagio '*Il Terremoto*' ('The Earthquake').

This refers to the earthquake at the moment of Christ's death recorded in Matthew 27:50–51. However, this section may also provide an important clue as to why Messia's service became popular in Europe in the latter part of the eighteenth century. This is because Messia is thought to have conceived the service in response to a devastating earthquake in Peru in 1687. At the time, this natural disaster was believed by many to be an act of divine retribution for the sins of the people of Peru, and so it is suggested that Messia initially held the service as an act of penitence on behalf of those who survived the earthquake. Messia's opening meditation would certainly resonate with penitent victims of an earthquake:

> All nature is disturbed at beholding the suffering of its Creator. The earth is covered with a thick darkness; an earthquake rends the rocks asunder, and bursts open the graves; the angels are horror-stricken at beholding their Lord in such cruel torments; the devils rage with anger, because the chastisement which men deserve for their sins is not immediately inflicted on them, as it was upon themselves.[3]

The European connection occurs because in 1755 a serious earthquake affected much of Portugal and Spain. The Lisbon earthquake of 1 November took place at 9.30 a.m. on a Sunday morning when many were attending church, and among the thousands of victims were large numbers of worshippers. This earthquake had a profound effect on the people of Europe, and particularly upon the Churches, which sought to come to terms with the circumstances of the devastation. Although Lisbon was worst affected, the earthquake's impact was widespread, and the port of Cadiz was struck by a tidal wave. Against this background, it is highly plausible that Messia's service would have found a place in the worship of a generation that bore the physical and psychological scars of a tsunami and who sought to make sense of this 'act of God'.

Whatever the reason for its introduction in Europe, the service

rapidly gained popularity. Soon those conducting the service produced their own addresses, and the success of Haydn's music led to a
different format to that devised by Messia being widely adopted. In
Messia's original format each address was followed by silence, the
recitation of appropriate verses, and prayers. In the new format,
following Haydn's example, each address was followed by music. It is
this combination of word and music that has proved popular and has
been widely used ever since, both in devotional services and concert
performances.

Haydn was not the first composer to find inspiration from the
seven last words. In the 1640s the German composer Schütz wrote an
oratorio on this theme, although this is more akin to a conventional
passion than a set of reflective pieces. Similarly, the seven last words
feature in Graun's *The Death of Jesus* (1755). Like Schütz and Graun,
many composers have reflected on the seven last words within orato-
rios or works based on Christ's passion, including Beethoven, Spohr,
Williams, Gounod, Stainer, Somervell and Mercandante. Others have
followed more closely Haydn's format, including Dubois, Cesar
Franck, Tournemire, Gubaidulina and, most recently, James
MacMillan and Ian Wilson, while a recording by American rock
musicians, *At the Foot of the Cross*, offers a strikingly different interpretation. Such a long history and wide variety of styles indicates what an
enduring and inspiring theme the seven last words have proved to be.

As well as music, numerous books of meditations on the seven last
words have been published – the British Library catalogue currently
lists well over a hundred. The theme has a widespread appeal across
Christian denominations and traditions. Within Catholicism, entering
Christ's suffering has long been regarded as a means of gaining
spiritual insight into what it means to 'take up your cross and follow
me'. From a Protestant perspective, the cross is revered as the means by
which Christ redeemed humanity. It is perhaps for these reasons that
the Good Friday Three Hours' Devotion has its roots in Catholicism,
but has become widespread among Protestant churches. Within the
Anglican Church, its first use was probably by the Victorian ritualist

the Revd A. H. Mackonochie, at St Alban's, Holborn, London, in 1864. The service soon became popular, and an account of the service at St Paul's, Knightbridge, in 1869, reported that, 'Hard-headed men of business, Members of Parliament, and many of both sexes, who are better known in the world of fashion than in the assembly of the sanctuary – were there.'[4] The first English cathedral to adopt the service was St Paul's in 1878.

The seven last words also appear from time to time in other forms of literature. John Donne's final sermon, delivered in 1630, draws a parallel between the seven last words and the seven days of the week. Gerard Manley Hopkins' seven 'terrible' sonnets are based on the seven last words. The seven last words appear in James Joyce's *Ulysses*, while in his *Stephen Hero* (an early version of *A Portrait of the Artist as a Young Man*), the main character attends a Three Hours' Devotion, after which he agonises over the seven last words. Dylan Thomas's poem 'Altarwise by Owl-light' paraphrases the seven last words, Samuel Beckett alludes to them in his play *Waiting for Godot,* as does Ted Hughes in 'The Seven Sorrows'. Such uses of, and references to, the seven last words indicate the profundity and emotional depth of these short phrases.

This book and CD draws on the Haydn format of Good Friday meditations of word and music. But rather than using the seven last words to focus inwards on Christ's suffering, together they offer a strikingly different and contemporary approach. Beginning with a chapter by Rowan Williams on the meaning of the cross in contemporary society, subsequent chapters take the form of a series of addresses in which each of the seven last words is the starting point to develop a thought-provoking and challenging reflection, offering insights into how the seven words can speak afresh in the early years of the twenty-first century. Each chapter relates to a track on the CD of music by Adrian Snell, who in over thirty years of composing, song-writing, performing and working as a music therapist, has explored the passion of Christ, the human condition and the Jewish roots of Christianity. After reading each chapter, readers are invited to reflect on what they have read using the music.

I first heard a three-hour meditation based on the seven last words as an ordinand at Cuddesdon Theological College, near Oxford, in the early 1960s. I found the preacher oppressive and, in order to maintain my equilibrium, let alone my faith, I slipped out and disappeared to the bottom of a nearby field to read Paul Tillich's *The Courage to Be*. This book, with its encouraging message that even in the most radical act of doubt there is an affirmation of faith, saved the day for me.

As a young curate in Hampstead, London, the three hours was an altogether different experience. It was delivered every year in the parish of Hampstead by the Revd Joseph McCulloch, the Rector of Mary-le-Bow. People came from all over London and virtually everyone stayed for the whole three hours. Always relating the seven last words to some other theme, such as Shakespeare's seven ages of man, the addresses were both enthralling and profound. We all came out feeling we had entered more deeply into the mystery both of Jesus and our own lives.

Having delivered Good Friday addresses a good number of times in the course of my own ministry there are two significant changes from those days. First, far more churches have a liturgy on Good Friday as well as addresses, so the actual time to meditate on the seven last words may be shorter. Second, as a result of biblical scholarship it is important and more helpful to draw out, through the words, the different insights of each evangelist. In short, rather than seeing the seven last words as a composite whole, it is good to stress the distinctive perspective of the different evangelists.

I commend this book and CD most warmly for use in personal meditation by individual Christians and as a source of inspiration for those who have to speak on Good Friday. In addition to Rowan Williams, whose writings are appreciated round the world, there is an interesting mixture of younger theologians with a strong shared desire to show how the seven last words which the evangelists report as Jesus having uttered on the cross relate to the concerns of the present century. The Welsh priest and poet R. S. Thomas once said in a BBC programme:

I think I am content to say I am a Christian because I think
Christianity, the Christian doctrine, is the most profound and
satisfactory answer to the great problem of suffering. [I don't
think] even in this late stage of the 20th century there is anything
more contemporary than the cross.[5]

The insights of this book, together with the accompanying music, will
bear out the truth of that remark.

The cross in the 21st century

ROWAN WILLIAMS

When Jesus of Nazareth was crucified, crosses were a daily sight. They reminded people who was in charge in Roman Palestine, what the cost was of offering any kind of challenge to the occupying power. When Jesus had encouraged his disciples to pick up their crosses and follow him, he was speaking with a kind of grim irony: if you're going to follow me, you should know that, one way or another, it's an act of rebellion, an act that will, one way or another, cost you your life. It was a live metaphor because it was so immediate a reality.

In the nearly two thousand years that have passed, language about crosses has become dead metaphor. The cross now lives only in religious language – whereas in the first century it represented things that were as far as you could imagine from religion. As Paul points out, the connection between crucifixion and God was shocking, tasteless and uncomfortable for Jews and non-Jews alike. But in a world where crosses are mainly seen in churches or around people's necks, what has happened to the original, difficult, transformative content of the language? How can the cross be talked about now in a way that makes a difference?

'Take up your cross' now means 'Put up with your minor discomforts', or, at most, 'Be sure that you do something to show God you take him seriously by making yourself uncomfortable in some way.' 'We all have our crosses to bear' means that we must all demonstrate perseverance in circumstances we don't fully control. The cross is as much a daily sight as it was in Jesus' day, but for a quite different reason: it has become a sign for something disconnected from the actual experiences of power and powerlessness, fear and hope, in society; it has become the marker of a minority-interest group, who seem to use it with rather obsessional frequency. If Jesus' Palestine was full of crosses, so is many a church; but the difference is plain.

It isn't an answer to this if we simply intensify the emotional charge of the religious symbol by stressing the extremity of the suffering depicted. That has been done pretty regularly since the late Middle Ages; it is still done by contemporary artists who are determined to shock. The truth is that we can find plenty of examples of extreme suffering (and people always have been able to find them), many of them more immediately effective for us than the image of the cruci-fied. And once we acknowledge that what we are looking for is just images of suffering, we might well ask a few questions about our motivation. The rather murky psychological background to some of the Christian fascination with the cross is hard to evade. Paul knew that the shock of the cross was not how badly Jesus suffered (what about those who lingered on the cross for days? What about the other ways in which a law-abiding empire tortured its non-citizens to death?), and we need, in thinking about the cross, to move beyond the attempt to bring emotions to the boil by pretending that this was, by definition, a uniquely awful form of physical pain.

There are two things we probably ought to hold in our minds if we want to understand afresh what meditation on the cross is properly for. The first is what we have already noted: in its context, the procla-mation of God's involvement in the cross says something about power and risk. The second is to do with what makes *this* cross, among all the others in its era, significant, world-changingly significant.

To walk with Jesus and to belong with the God of Jesus is risky; but not in the simple sense that you might become a martyr for the divine cause. That's bearable, even attractive to a certain mindset. We hardly need reminding of that in today's world of suicide bombers. The majority of those crucified in Roman Judea and Galilee were not in fact modern freedom fighters but a mixture of petty thugs, delinquent or runaway slaves and innocents executed for the purposes of plain state terror. The crucified is literally nailed up as a notice of what the powerful mean to say; the crucified is not a martyr but more of a cypher, a naked and more or less anonymous signifier in the language of someone else (the governing authority). The cross is not about extremity of suffering so much as extremity of helplessness, impotence in speaking what *you* mean to say.

To walk with Jesus and the God of Jesus, then, is to risk having nothing to say that power can hear, to risk becoming a cypher in someone else's scheme of things. This is why it is not just politically correct sentimentality to imagine the meaning of the cross in relation to the experience of a raped woman or an abused child. Again and again we are told that the anguish here is so often that of being deprived of any way of describing what has happened except in terms of the story told by the possessor of power: the woman or the child is pre-emptively seen as the one who provokes desire and so shares responsibility for the act which invades and silences them.

The cross is where the non-citizens are executed; it defines the fact, much thought about by the earliest Christians, that belonging with the God of Jesus is the opposite of being a citizen, someone with clear, publicly agreed rights and status. The 'rights' of the Christian are grounded in active relation with God and each other rather than the law of the state. And this is not simply a transition into a mildly utopian community alongside the state (as if coming to belong with Jesus were like joining CND or the Green Party); it is to invite the unwelcome fate of being written out of the story, having no meaning that the public sphere can grasp. This has nothing to do with any kind of commendation by the powerful to the powerless to accept their doubtless disagreeable lot. It is an observation that in a society where non-citizens can be painfully and fairly casually slaughtered, God is not a citizen; so that if we are to be found where God is, we can't stay safely within our citizen's rights.

So recovering the sense of what the cross is about involves us first in some reflection on becoming a non-citizen alongside God. The cross is a gateway into that strange community in which non-citizens belong together because they belong with God. God in the cross accepts the fate of being silenced, deprived of the words to utter his own meaning. But this is not to say that God expects us to be silenced by the murderous injustice of the world. To be unequivocally with him is to be stripped of the ordinary ways of making sense, stripped of what might carry weight in the world's frame of reference. But to be with him is also to be with all who are, by their choice or the choice of others, non-citizens, non-belongers; it is to be part of a social order that depends on nothing but God's presence and self-gift, God's decision to be with the non-belongers. It is this vision that makes the writer of the Letter to the Hebrews encourage believers to go to where Jesus is 'outside the camp', looking for a 'city' that doesn't yet exist (13:3–14). And looking for a non-existent city is rather more than accepting passively a situation of oppression; it is to be involved in building and sustaining alternatives to the way the world makes sense.

Following Jesus leads to where God is; following Jesus leads to places where people are robbed of their speech and their social power. God is to be discovered where social power runs out, as the reality that has nothing in common with social power. Only with this in mind can we grasp how the cross begins to be the act of creating a new communal phenomenon, sufficiently new and peculiar to be still, two thousand years on, tantalisingly hard to describe and constantly trying to evade its own distinctiveness. The cross is where Christian distinctiveness is focused – not because Christianity is first and foremost a religion of suffering, but because it is a social reality constituted by the strange impact of divine action in the death of someone by this particular method which is associated with the slave and the non-citizen.

But all this relates to the second theme mentioned, the question of what makes *this* crucifixion different and decisive. The answer is already there in essence. This is the crucifixion of someone who claims to speak for God. To follow him, he has said, is to be with God; his words and actions, he says or implies, are a renewal of God's call to God's people, widening out the definition of who may be part of God's people with a startling disregard for the conventional interpretation of acceptable criteria for this. He promises being with God and his path leads to the cross; so that we are starkly challenged as to whether we can cope with identifying this place of execution as God's place.

In the light of Jesus' words and actions, the crucifixion is the drastic rejection of God's action, God's call. What is crucified is the embodiment of divine promise or grace, which is nailed up as superfluous, threatening, empty and lethally dangerous all at once by those who cannot hear what promise means. It is true to say that God is crucified. And once again, we should be cautious about turning this simply into a drama of suffering – the transcendent God at last experiencing human woe, rather like a King Lear deprived of his royalty and 'feeling what wretches feel'. This has a certain emotional force, but it can also be a sentimental projection. What is done on the cross is not about the intensity with which God feels human sorrow (a coherent doctrine of God ought to have told us already that the God of the First Covenant knows precisely what human grief and loss are; if he needs to become incarnate to know it, something odd is being said about both the nature of God and the Hebrew Scriptures). It is about where God *is*; and about what human hatred and self-hatred actually means.

The rejection of Jesus is the rejection of an unconditional promise of God's fellowship. And this is not simply saying no to a potentially attractive but finally optional human good; if human beings are made in God's likeness and designed to share the divine life in some sense, the rejection of Jesus is the rejection of humanity itself by humanity. The cross is the human imagination cutting off the branch it is sitting on, trying to pull up its own roots. And so we can make some further connections. To stand with God is to stand with those who don't belong; but those who don't belong may be found on the cross, dying the death of a slave. God is the author of the invitation to life itself, and more specifically of the invitation to life in the company of Jesus as the one who assures us concretely and historically of our divine welcome; God creates a kind of belonging without analogues in the 'natural' world. And so to refuse to stand where Jesus is is to push against the very grain of creation, to deny what I am created to be, to decline to belong with God. Yet God has chosen to belong with us; and if we refuse to belong with him, he is still to be found with us in our self-rejection or self-exclusion, since he cannot define his position as another sort of 'ordinary' belonging with its conditions and limitations.

The crucified Jesus is not only the God who stands with the non-citizen; he also tells me that my refusals of his invitation are self-destructive – and that therefore the way I desire to keep at a distance from those who don't belong are a self-deprivation, ultimately a self-refusal.

Here it is in the lines of Charles Causley's poem, 'I Am the Great Sun. From a Normandy crucifix of 1632':

> I am the great sun, but you do not see me,
> I am your husband, but you turn away…
> I am your counsel, but you do not hear me,
> I am the lover whom you will betray,
> I am the victor, but you do not cheer me,
> I am the holy dove whom you will slay.
> I am your life, but if you will not name me,
> Seal up your soul with tears, and never blame me.[1]

Reflecting on the cross in the contemporary world is, I've been suggesting, more than just thinking about the inescapable realities of tragedy or about God's involvement with suffering. It is the painful process of taking up a stance, 'staking yourself' in Gillian Rose's favoured phrase. Understood as the distinctive word of an active God, the cross invites us to ask where we stand, with whom; and to ask what we have done to ourselves in the whole human record of mutual refusal and rejection. We are confronted with the fact of God's stance, God's self-staking, in such a way that we cannot escape the conclusion that the violence of human refusal is suicidal. The death I collude with, the death and silencing of the one with no rights, no citizenship, is *my* death because it is God's death, the death God has chosen to make his own so as to speak to us and act for us and upon us.

From the very first, believers have seen the cross as an action, not only a passion, something done, not only the record of things done *to* someone. Hence the cry of triumph, 'It is finished', at the climax of St John's story of the crucifixion. The cross is the end of Jesus' journey in the name and power of God to where people are deprived of humanity – by suffering oppression, by being silenced, but also by their own fear and withdrawal. It completes the picture of how God's transforming love works by showing us where that love can be seen. It is the sign and the substance of God's decision to be where his human creation tries hardest to kill itself. At precisely the point where we exercise most energy and ingenuity in attempting to dig up our roots in God's creative love, that love reasserts itself.

Hence it makes sense to speak of the cross as the paying of a price: the bearer of God's life bears the consequence of human self-hatred, the cost of human fear. What is unique on the cross of Jesus is not either some special intensity of agony or some abstract transaction to placate God's justice. It is the fact that this death, this slave's death, is carried by the one who has consistently and unbrokenly carried God's absolute promise in every act and word of his. As in the gospel of John, it is as if people were being invited to express their fear and hatred in unprecedentedly direct form: *here* is the mercy of God; *this* is what you hate and fear when you hate and fear each other. And by bearing this in God's name and power, the cross creates a different kind of citizenship by its invitation to belong with the God of non-belongers.

So we reflect on the words from the cross in the light of this central word: here is where God has chosen to be. Here is where the barriers are broken down between God and the darkest places of the human mind; and so here too is where the barriers are down between human beings. The death of Jesus on the cross marks the creation of an unbreakable alliance, a covenant, between God and humanity, made visible in the covenant community: entering the community is by choosing to be where Christ is in his death (baptism), participation is bound up with eating and drinking together in the faith that the common nourishment of bread and wine is in fact nourishment with the life that on the cross expressed the desire of God to be in the world like *this*.

Here is where God has chosen to be. But this is not a matter of human imagination recognising God through this shocking event by some great leap of intuitive perception. Christians have understood the resurrection as God's 'indication' of his presence on the cross. The resurrection is God displaying the crucified body to us, saying that here in this wounded body is still where he lives and speaks. It is so often remarked that the risen Jesus in the gospels does not appear as a glorified and resplendent body but as the one who – visibly – has suffered death. He is recognised by his wounds. What is being said is not only that God's love is undefeated by human rejection, but that this love continues to embody itself exactly as in Jesus' ministry – that ministry which leads inexorably to the slave's death. There is no way around or behind the 'form of the slave' to a smoother or calmer version of what divine love means, no way of internalising that love into our own feelings of comfort and acceptance. The divine love made flesh continues to be the love that is visible of the cross of the non-citizen, with all that means for our own conversion and incorporation into the community of the non-citizens.

The resurrection 'displays' the cross – but not as an ideal or an abstract summons to individual faith. It displays the body of the crucified as alive, and as (in the way it was before) the concrete place of God's call to reconciliation with God and each other. To pick up Paul's imagery, the crucified body is the throne in the Holy of Holies, the *kapporeth* where atonement is made. But it is in the light of the resurrection that this can be seen and said, because the resurrection is the manifesting of the fact that God *continues* to choose to be where the crucified Jesus is, and thus makes the crucified Jesus alive as body, as person.

Reflecting on the cross does not, for the believer, simply begin with the cross as an historical event; it begins from recognising – as a result of God's act in the resurrection – what is unique in this cross as well as what in the cross is the universal truth of our untruthful humanity. It begins with recognising that this is the place where God and humanity are displayed in equal clarity and fullness. It is the ultimately irreligious place; and at the same time the Holy of Holies. It changes what holiness means because it changes our estimate of where God is. And if we are serious about it, it changes not simply what we think or feel, but literally where we are, where we find ourselves.

A meditation

So where am I?

I'm terrified of finding myself there because I can't cope with not being able to make sense. I want to be talking the same language as others. After all, how shall I witness to God if I'm talking in terms no one understands?

I know that I'm supposed to believe that this is where God chooses to be, but I don't believe it. God is full of compassion for the lost, the non-belongers, the non-citizens, but he's still God, after all, and he must surely want me to be who I am in effective and sensible ways, so that I can point people to his transcendence.

And all he will say to me is, 'Here is your life, and nowhere else.' He says, 'I don't ask you first to be effective and eloquent; first I ask you to be where I am and to be alive. You can spend all the years of your life struggling to be an effective witness for me, but if you haven't been here with me you are not yet alive.'

It looks as though what I hate is the thought of being alive; just being where he is, irrespective of what I have done or can do or have said or can say. And I hate the thought of being alive only with, only alongside, those who have turned their backs on success or who have already 'lost' in whatever battles there are to be fought.

I don't know if I can cope with there being no battles to win, with God having already dissolved that whole frame of reference. And I'm not sure I want life that can only be lived in such company.

I die because I will not die. I seal up my soul with tears because I will not take the step to where God is and join God's company, so long as the cost is what it is.

And I'm not even sure what the first step might be to where God is.

Perhaps if I could just see the nearest and most obvious non-citizen in whom God calls to me; if I could just see where the boundaries were that I must cross here and now…

I want to see because I do want life. No I don't, I want it on my solitary terms. Yes I do, because I see how people die like that. I'm at war with myself; who will deliver me from this body condemned to die?

I want and I don't want; I see and I don't see. Give me time, God, give me strength to want with the centre of myself. Give me room in my heart for the truth I think I hate and know I love.

Part Two
Seven Words for Three Hours

*A Good Friday Meditation
in Words and Music*

At the sixth hour

It's the sixth hour. In the heat of the midday sun we stand at the foot of a cross. We have come to watch and wait as followers of one of the executed.

We stand alongside those who have come to witness a spectacle – the grim fascination of suffering and death. We stand alongside the anguished families and friends of those hanging on crosses. We stand alongside soldiers, dispassionately marshalling events.

We know the story. We know why he is there. But this familiarity doesn't change our mood, or our feelings of anger, grief and helplessness.

As his followers, we also want to hear what he may say – what his last words to us will be. We know they will be special. We know we will treasure them. We know they will speak to us afresh each time we recall them and this moment.

And so we watch, and wait, and pray, and listen …

Music: Track 1 'The World is Full of Tears'

'Father, forgive them; for they know not what they do' (Luke 23:34)

EDMUND NEWELL

A man sits at a table. Before him are two scrolls. Patiently and carefully, he copies the words of one scroll onto the other. As he writes, he thinks and prays about the words he copies. This is no laborious chore, it's an act of loving devotion.

The words he's copied so far have confused, challenged, excited and inspired him. But now his mood has darkened. As the story before him unfolds, it's taken him to the crucifixion of the one about whom he writes. Although the execution took place many years before, it could have been only yesterday. All that he sees are words, but in his mind's eye the writer witnesses the terrible event.

The reason for such emotional intensity is that the person nailed to the cross dominates the writer's life: his prayers, his relationships, his judgements, his hopes and expectations. All that he does – all that he is – is in reference to that person.

What will he write next? Looking down he sees that the completed scroll continues, 'And they cast lots to divide his clothing.' But another phrase has come to mind, a familiar phrase ascribed to that man on the cross and handed down by reliable witnesses: 'Father forgive them; for they know not what they do.'

He pauses. His sheer revulsion at the crucifixion pushes away thoughts of forgiveness – instead, the image evokes feelings of powerlessness, frustration, hatred and revenge. And yet that phrase in his mind will not go away. It pulls him in another direction, challenging his instinctive feelings – just like so much he knows about that man. That compassionate, understanding, forgiving phrase seems so apt for the man about whom he writes – the man who gives meaning to his life.

He has a choice and must make a decision. What should he write next?

Many years ago, a scribe copying Luke's gospel may have faced this dilemma, for the first of the seven last words doesn't appear in some of the earliest manuscripts. These words were either removed from or added to the original version by a scribe. Why? The simple answer is that we don't know. Whatever the explanation the question remains: who is it that Jesus prays for?

We might reasonably assume he's praying for the Roman soldiers. After all, they were simply acting under orders to crucify a convicted criminal. But in Luke's account of events it's not the Romans who are held accountable for Christ's crucifixion, it's 'the Jews' – both the religious leaders and the crowd. And so it seems that Christ's prayer of forgiveness was either removed because of strong anti-Jewish feelings, or added to counter hostility towards the Jews. Both explanations make sense given what's known of the often tense relationship between Jews and Christians at the time.

The sad truth is that as Christianity broke away from its Jewish roots, considerable hostility was shown by some Christians towards Jews, and vice versa. As the largely Gentile Christian Church emerged, a bitter hatred towards the Jewish people surfaced within certain sections of it. From what started out as sibling rivalry within the Jewish family – for Christianity's origins are Jewish – something far more sinister emerged and anti-Judaism took hold. This was the start of a troubled history of relations between Christians and Jews that has lasted for centuries.

When people are exposed for the first time to the history of anti-Judaism within the Church they are shocked, as it seems so much at odds with the Christian ethic of loving one's neighbour. What's more, it soon becomes apparent that the Church's teaching and actions over hundreds of years may well have helped create the conditions that made the Holocaust possible. This, too, is a shocking realisation.

So there is an urgency not to forget the past but to learn the lessons of this troubled history. This is not only vital to ensure good relations between Christians and Jews today, but to understand how religious faith can be tainted and become a vehicle for harm – and how we can unwittingly be caught up in it. Christ's prayer from the cross therefore speaks to us now, as it has spoken through the ages, for each generation through its ignorance and folly is in need of God's forgiveness. The Christ who died for us all prays for us all.

For Christians of all traditions, Good Friday is a profoundly moving and solemn day. Yet many Christians are not aware of the sad irony that for many centuries Good Friday was a day of fear for Jewish people. From an early stage in the Church's history 'the Jews' were collectively blamed for Christ's death, and so were often attacked on the very day Christians recollect the crucifixion most powerfully, Good Friday.

Such attacks didn't merely express mindless mob hatred towards a religious minority. Some of the most revered theologians and leaders of the early Church fuelled hostility. In 338 a synagogue in Callinicum in Syria was burnt down. St Ambrose responded, 'it was I who set fire to the synagogue; indeed I gave orders for it to be done so that there should no longer be any place where Christ is denied.'[1] In 387 in Antioch in Syria, St John Chrysostom delivered a series of sermons known as *Against the Jews* in which he argued that 'demons dwell in the synagogue not only in the place itself, but in the souls of the Jews'.[2] In the fifth century, St Augustine wrote that Jews were scattered throughout the world without a homeland and destined to suffer as a punishment and as witness that Christianity had superseded Judaism – hence our phrase 'wandering Jew'. Down the centuries, in the name of Christianity, Jews have suffered mass slaughter, expulsion from countries, social ostracism, forced conversion and baptism, and bans on entering certain trades and professions or receiving education.

But why - why this assault on God's 'Chosen People'?

An important reason is that the New Testament contains many negative statements about 'the Jews'. The most dangerous is the so-called 'blood curse' in Matthew's gospel, when Pilate addresses the Jewish crowd at Christ's trial saying, 'I am innocent of this man's blood; see to it yourselves', to which they reply, 'His blood be on us and on our children!' (27:24–25). From this, the Jews have been collectively blamed for deicide – killing God – and Christians throughout history have seen Jews as tainted by the sin of their forebears.

There can be little doubt that centuries of hatred of the Jews fuelled by both Protestants and Catholics helped to set the scene for anti-Semitism and the Holocaust. There are even some chilling parallels between Hitler's actions and those of the Church. It was the Roman Church that first required Jews to wear yellow badges to distinguish them from non-Jews, and to segregate them in what later became known as ghettos. Both practices were reintroduced by the Nazis in 1939. Perhaps most disturbing of all was Hitler's appeal to the reformer Martin Luther's chilling remark, 'if they [the Jews] turn from their blasphemies, we must surely forgive them; but if not, we must not suffer them to remain.' What's more, Luther's 'advice' 'that their synagogues should be burnt down' has a chilling parallel with the anti-Jewish riots of *Kristallnacht* on 9 and 10 November 1938, which is regarded by many as the beginning of the Holocaust.

To appreciate the influence of anti-Judaism among Christians one need look no further than to Dietrich Bonhoeffer. He is rightly remembered for his brave opposition to Nazism, the help that he gave to the victims of the Nazi regime – including Jews – and his involvement in the failed plot to assassinate Hitler, which led to his arrest and execution. The courageous and scholarly Bonhoeffer, whose statue on the west front of Westminster Abbey recognises him as one of the great Christian martyrs of the twentieth century, was considered for honour as a 'Righteous among the nations' at the Yad Vashem Holocaust Memorial in Jerusalem. And yet, as state anti-Semitism took hold in Germany, Bonhoeffer commented in a lecture in 1933:

> The [German] State's measures against Jewry are connected, however, in a very special way with the Church. In the Church of Christ we have never lost sight of the idea that the 'chosen people', which placed the Saviour of the World on the Cross, must bear the curse of its actions through a long history of suffering.[3]

Such a statement sits uncomfortably with Bonhoeffer's later acts of compassion and bravery on behalf of the Jews, and one can only speculate as to how his thinking developed as the full horror of anti-Semitism became clear. Significantly for us, it shows also how even a compassionate and deep-thinking person of faith can be influenced by a church culture steeped in prejudice.

The Holocaust has been picked over from many angles. From the Christian perspective, the systematic destruction of six million people finally brought the Church to its knees and to it senses. During the Second World War, the Council of Christians and Jews came into being, to promote good relations and better understanding. In 1965, the Roman Catholic Church redefined its attitude to Judaism. This change was no better symbolised than when Pope John Paul II, on his visit to Jerusalem in 2000, placed a piece of paper on the Western Wall – that holiest of sites for Jews. The paper contained a prayer for forgiveness for what the Church has done down the ages to those he called 'the people of the Covenant'. In the same year, a new script was written for the world-famous Oberammagau Play, which Hitler once described as showing 'the whole muck and mire of Jewry'.[4] The new production emphasises the Jewishness of Jesus and his disciples, and the controversial blood curse has been removed.

Where should we go from here?

In churches every week passages are read from the New Testament that include negative statements about 'the Jews' – John's gospel alone contains over seventy. Put them in context. Keep in mind that Christianity started as a Jewish movement. Remember it argued with other Jewish groups. As you ponder this sibling rivalry, think of the harsh things that Christians of different traditions say about each other today – not least within the Anglican Communion. In the heat of the argument we tend to demonise the opposition unnecessarily. But in our more prayerful moments we recognise the deep value and importance of staying in relationship – because God is in relationship with all.

Christians also need to learn that the Church has persecuted the Jews through history, and how our bishops and priests fuelled and justified this – it will help us to be sensitive to how our faith can be a tool of abuse even today. We would do well to remember this in the current climate, where it is so easy for Islamophobia to take hold. We must beware of projecting our fear of extremist Islamic terrorists onto all Muslims – and of demonising their faith. Our history shows where that can lead.

Christians can also remember the Jewish roots of their faith – and celebrate it. For example, when churches commission works of art, the use of Jewish imagery can help to emphasise the interconnectedness of the two faiths, as can the use of Jewish prayers in Christian liturgy. So often it is when other cultures no longer seem alien to us that we feel comfortable with them and better relationships are fostered.

It was the British writer William Norman Ewer who in the 1920s wrote this clerihew:

> How odd
> Of God
> To choose
> The Jews

To which Cecil Browne famously replied:

> But not so odd
> As those who choose
> A Jewish God
> But spurn the Jews.

The spurning of Jews by Christians for many centuries is more than an oddity, it is both a scandal and a tragedy. It is also a warning – a warning of how a religion whose core ethic is of love and forgiveness can harbour and justify prejudice and hatred.

It is only of late, with the benefit of biblical scholarship, that the anti-Jewish statements in the New Testament have been seen in their true context, as part of an internal struggle within communities of faith. Uncomfortable as they may be, they make sense in this context. Taken out of context they become divisive and dangerous.

Christ's first words from the cross also need to be placed in context. But unlike those words of hostility and mistrust, they have a timeless quality, and they challenge us now to obey God's will. Like the scribe of Luke's gospel, we often struggle to understand what God asks of us. The question is, in seeking to obey God's will, will we learn from past mistakes, and will the lessons of the past help us come to our senses before we need to pray, 'Father forgive us, we know not what we do'?

Music: Track 2 'Kaddish for Bergen-Belsen'

'Truly, I say to you, today you will be with me in Paradise' (Luke 23:43)

GILES FRASER

A bullfight, a war film, a boxing match or a public crucifixion: what are the ethics of 'watching'? Of course, we are never *just* watching. So what is the extent to which watching is participating? At what point do we become complicit? For surely we must watch the news, however terrible, and face the horror and violence that exists in our world. Likewise, there are films and novels that, through their depiction of violence, help us understand more fully its nature and reality so as to confront it. But when does the depiction of violence become a pornography of violence?

The term 'pornoviolence' was coined in the 1960s in response to a spate of movies such as *Bonnie and Clyde* and *The Dirty Dozen* that combined extremes of violence with entertainment in an unprecedented way – or at least, in a way that was unprecedented in the film industry. For the combination of violence and entertainment is an ancient one that takes us back, not just to the Colosseum but also to the foot of the cross itself.

Whatever else it was, crucifixion was a spectacle, designed to be seen. The suffering body is held up high, in a public place, carefully staged for maximum effect. Christ is crucified alongside two criminals. And people came from far and wide just to watch.

Is that form of voyeurism so different from watching a movie? For it is at the movies that our position as voyeur is most acute. We sit in the dark. We can see but we are not ourselves seen. From this vantage point we have an access to those parts of life usually deemed especially private. From the dark we see people making love and people dying, and all in such minute detail or slow motion. How, then, does watching a film affect us?

Imagine for a moment that you are in a cinema. In the darkness you are watching a film. There are fights. There are deaths. There is brutality. Does the film make violence seem innocuous or acceptable? Do you find the realism of the violence shocking or entertaining, or even amusing?

Imagine the characters. There are some you like and some you dislike. How does the film-maker elicit your sympathies? Are they elicited in such a way as to make you feel comfortable or uncomfortable about the experience of watching?

Try to disrupt the spell cast by all the narrative and cinematic tricks. Spin different imaginative tales. If there is a casual death, imagine a family for that person, imagine them as a child.

One of the most controversial films of recent years, and one destined to be shown time and time again on Good Friday, is Mel Gibson's *The Passion of the Christ*. This is a disturbing film. For those who can stomach it, the film shows in gory detail and at considerable length what being beaten up, scourged and crucified is like. It shows what Christ, the thieves alongside him, and many others, probably went through when they were executed. But it is disturbing not only for its violence. More problematic is how it relates the realism of suffering to the film's narrative – a hybrid created from gospel accounts, later traditions and the director's imagination. Because of its realism in one respect, we could be lulled into thinking that the whole film is unusually accurate: 'It is as it was', as Pope John Paul II was apparently wrongly reported to have said about it.

For instance, the film's sympathetic portrayal of Pilate – who we know from non-biblical sources was a harsh and brutal Governor – is implausible. By portraying Pilate in this way, the film directs the responsibility for Christ's crucifixion towards the Jewish religious leaders and crowd who pressurised a reluctant Governor. As voyeurs of this unfolding tragedy, we are led to feel sympathy towards Pilate and anger towards the religious leaders and the mob. With it, we are in danger of being drawn into the pitfalls discussed in the first address.

Another film that provided its director not only with a box-office hit but an outlet to explore deeply held convictions is Stephen Spielberg's *Schindler's List*. Based on a book by Thomas Keneally, *Schindler's List* tells the story of how the German war profiteer Oscar Schindler came to save more than a thousand Jews from the death camps, risking his life and losing his fortune in the process. The film won seven academy awards and received huge popular acclaim. It has been widely used in schools as a teaching aid and consequently, for a whole generation, *Schindler's List* has become one of the most influential points of access for understanding the horrors of the Holocaust.

A number of critics, however, have faulted the film's oversimplification of complex moral issues. The reviewer Bryan Cheyette calls it 'a seductive and self-confident narrative' that has 'no real understanding of the difficulties inherent in representing the ineffable'.[1] He's not alone in wanting to claim that the Holocaust is so utterly terrible that nothing is able to capture its horror, that we are forced into silence by its very magnitude. The German philosopher Theodor Adorno famously asserted there could be no more poetry after Auschwitz. We need to cry not speak. The Holocaust, like the cross itself, leads many of us into silence.

But there are very real problems with the silence too. Imagine the following: I am out at the supermarket and I see a neighbour coming towards me. I know that she has just lost a child in a tragic cot death. Panic sets in. What do I say? What is there to say? Better to say nothing than come out with embarrassed clichés. So I slip down the next aisle and pass by unnoticed. Silence seems somehow altogether more profound than nervous chatter. And yet, of course, it is my blushes that are being spared here. It is my fear at confronting the pain of cot death that leads me to silence. For silence can also be yet one more form of avoidance, a subtle and persuasive strategy to help us overlook the horror.

We often sit in silence before the cross. And for many of us silence is the only appropriate response to its horror. We have nothing to say. Silence is respectful. Not only that, it somehow seems that only silence has the sort of gravitas that can match the seriousness of the subject. On occasions, though, silence can reflect a false piety purchased far too cheaply. Too often something has not been faced. But what? In the liturgy of Holy Week we begin by welcoming Christ into the city. Often the congregation are cast as the crowd: 'Hosanna in the highest!' we cry out. It is this self-same crowd who will be jeering and spitting before the week is out: 'Crucify him!' What is hard for us to face is the suspicion that we too would have betrayed Christ in similar circumstances. We can sit before the cross and think how terrible it is that *they* have murdered *our* Lord. Or one can count oneself among the murderers, swept up in the frenzy of the mob, too afraid to speak out, ready to go along with what the authorities decide.

In a famous scene from the film, Schindler witnesses the liquidation of the ghetto. He sits astride his horse on a hill overlooking the ghetto and is horrified by the brutality and violence unfolding before him. Prompted by his girlfriend, he has to look away. And that's my/our reaction too: I feel ill and want to hide behind the sofa. Like Schindler, the viewer watches the film from some safe distance. And that, precisely, is the problem with this film. For all its dramatic realism about the horrors of human suffering, Schindler's List is a feel-good film. Though we may cry and be appalled by the brutality of Nazi genocide, the place from which we watch the film is never fully challenged. We are not asked to examine our own potential for viciousness, we are never provoked to think whether we too would have become a camp bully or a silent coward. The perspective from the sofa, like that from the hilltop promontory, is sheltered from the threat of moral or spiritual interrogation. As the philosopher Gillian Rose put it, from the sofa 'our complacency is left in place and willfully reinforced'.

Part of what is at stake here is our frequent refusal to face our own potential for wickedness. In her excellent book called *Wickedness*, Mary Midgely writes:

> We try to avoid 'owning' our bad motives, not just from vanity (though this is important) but because we feel that to own or acknowledge is to accept. We dread exposure to the hidden force whose power we sense. Our official idea of ourselves has no room for it.[2]

Self-deception arises 'because we see motives which are in fact our own as alien to us and refuse to acknowledge them'.[3] Instead we invent stories where the wickedness is embodied by an-other: an alien, a monstrous other, a foreigner, a Nazi with a funny accent. In refusing to acknowledge our 'shadow' – to use Jungian vocabulary – we give it more power, the power of working unchecked in the dark. Sometimes that darkness is called silence – the place beyond interrogation.

The great story of the dangers of self-avoidance is Robert Louis Stevenson's *The Strange Case of Dr Jekyll and Mr Hyde*. The story is, in part, about the dangers of pious self-righteousness. Dr Jekyll so refuses to acknowledge his darker side that it takes on a life of its own beyond the confines of his own self-image. Jekyll's concern for his own good character gives him no room to acknowledge his own Hyde-like tendencies. Consequently, they go unchecked: Mr Hyde is a consequence of Dr Jekyll's vanity. Similarly, we are commonly so unwilling to face our own potential for wickedness that, instead of squaring up to it and challenging it, we simply try to forget it or pretend it isn't there. This means that the dangerous part of ourselves is able to work unchecked. The appropriate and necessary 'crisis of identity' comes when one discovers Jekyll and Hyde are different sides to the same person – and not two different people.

In *Schindler's List* we are presented with two archetypes, Oskar Schindler and Amon Goeth. Like the two thieves crucified alongside Christ, these two represent, as it were, the good criminal and the bad criminal. Schindler, the war profiteer who gives all his money away to save his Jewish workforce, and Goeth, the suave camp commandant for whom murder is entertainment. In many ways Schindler and Goeth are portrayed as being very similar: both enjoy money, women, parties, good food. As Gillian Rose put it, 'they are said to be each other's "dark brother"'.[4] We could go further and say they are not only brothers, but one – a Jekyll and Hyde, one the shadow of the other.

Christian people are, I think, often particularly susceptible to this sort of splitting. We are supposed to be good, kind and gentle, etc. Our official self-image has no room for an acknowledgement of our own greedy, petty, revengeful secrets. There is a certain sort of 'Christian smile' that should make us shudder. For this smile is frequently a telltale sign of the presence of Mr Hyde.

One of the most challenging recent accounts of the Holocaust is that of Christopher Browning in his book *Ordinary Men*.[5] These 'ordinary men' were not career Nazis or Goeth-type psychopaths, they were policemen, too old to be of much use to the army. They were, as it were, you and I. And yet, in the July of 1942, Reserve Police Battalion 101 came to the Polish village of Józefów and shot some fifteen hundred Jews, mostly women, children and the elderly.

Two things are extraordinary about this account. The first is the permission Major Trapp gave for his soldiers to absent themselves from the bloody task ahead. What is even more extraordinary, however, is that only 'some ten or twelve' initially came forward out of a group of roughly five hundred 'ordinary men'. More men dropped out as the day's murder progressed, but even so, only about 10 per cent of the Battalion declined to go on. And this, of course, raises the question about the other 90 per cent. Often we imagine that many went along with orders out of fear for their own safety or that of their families. But this does not seem to have been a factor here. Given the lack of coercion, why did so many of these 'ordinary men' participate in the murders at Józefów? The book ends with the chilling question: 'If the men of Reserve Police Battalion 101 could become killers under such circumstances, what group of men cannot?'

How can we make best use of 'info-tainment'? The sort of film Gillian Rose wants about the Holocaust would work so as to reveal our own complicity in the patterns of life and thought that make the Holocaust possible. It is a film that encourages us to empathise with a member of the SS, where we are led to 'identify with his hopes and fears, disappointments and rage, so that when it comes to killing, we put our hands on the trigger with him, wanting him to get what he wants'. Of course, the problem with this sort of film is that we now know, in advance, how the story of the SS man will go and so our identification with such a character would be easy to resist. The same, of course, is true of the sort of film we might like to make about the crucifixion. In it we are led to identify with Pilate, but not Mel Gibson's sanitised Pilate. We are encouraged to see things from his point of view, we are shown the forces that motivate him. And when it comes to the moment of condemnation, we also wash our hands and turn our backs.

This is for another time. For the moment we wait, in prayer, at the foot of the cross. We do so not as voyeurs of Christ's suffering, watching from the dark and safe place, but observing all that takes place through the difficult and painful lens of self-critical vigilance. Such exploration is uncomfortable. But without the self-critical vigilance of the thief that begged Jesus for pardon, we may be complicit – however reluctant – in harm. For much harm has been done, and continues to be done, by those who feel removed from responsibility. This moment is our passion as well as Christ's.

Music: Track 3 'Burdens of Guilt'

'Woman, behold your son! ... Behold your mother!'

(John 19:26f)

LUCY WINKETT

'I'm spiritual but I'm not religious,' so many people say. It was the England soccer captain and husband of Posh Spice, David Beckham, who famously said of one of their sons, 'I have a sense of spirituality. I want Brooklyn christened but I don't know into what religion yet.'[1]

It has become a cliché to say that many people in modern affluent societies are searching for deeper meaning. Organised religion, no longer the first port of call for a generation unfamiliar with Christian language or stories, is not clear how to respond. As the theologian Dorothee Soelle has noted, in the West Christianity is regarded by the majority as almost irrelevant except as a purveyor and preserver of cultural memory.[2]

Two concerns often float to the surface as the problem with organised religion. The first concern is widely held, although only young people dare say it. In our entertainment-sodden culture, the church commits a serious sin: it's boring.

The second concern is more existential. The Church is a gathering, a community of the people of God. And this can seem precisely the problem. Spiritually hungry people sometimes wander into church. They are searching for meaningful experience. They are not ready to make a commitment, either of faith or of affiliation to a community. Yet they find themselves at once at risk of being asked to produce cakes for a sale; they are asked opinions on church linens or recruited to one side or another of a petty personality conflict. It's not that different from the world outside the church door. In organised religion the other people of God, it would seem, create the biggest distraction from the worship of God.

These two concerns are not conclusive or comprehensive but they capture some of the frustration expressed about religion by many inside and outside the Church. One is about the transcendent experience of worship, the other concerning the all too incarnational nature of human community. This word from the cross has something to say to each of these concerns.

Our first concern is that church is boring. This is not just worship, although it can include worship of any kind or any church tradition. Being bored is not the worst thing that can happen to a person so it's important not to get too carried away into a liturgical land of gimmicks and posters for an 'all-singing, all-dancing Eucharist on ice'. What makes an experience of church *not* boring is not distraction or diversion but authenticity.

In this sense, the opposite of 'boring' is not 'interesting' in a way that we may be able to assent to intellectually. The glory and beauty of an authentic spiritual community is less interesting than captivating; less distracting than compelling. What we seek in church is not a diverting experience to keep our mind and body occupied for an hour or so, but a saviour who will come looking for us, gather us up, throw us over his shoulder and take us home.

Mary and John stand looking up at Jesus. Jesus looks at them, and says: 'Behold. Behold one another. Look.' It's reminiscent of the time when Peter, James and John gazed on his face in wonder at the top of Mount Tabor; when his face shone and was transfigured. We will return to the contemplative aspect of this word from the cross later, but for now, it is the possibility of transfiguring the faces of those he loved in the midst of his agony that concerns us.

Mary and John would never be the same again; and the movement within them and between them was not so much a change of address, but a transfiguration.

A transfiguring experience is anything but boring. It is nothing less than transfiguration that is the measure of life together in our church communities.

There is no blueprint plan or series of changes that we can make to make transfiguration a natural part of our church life. We can't make it happen; but we can look for clues, signs of the movement of the transfiguring word of God in the world around us.

The Russian philosopher Nicholas Berdyaev thought a lot about the future of humanity and the authenticity of experience from the perspective of faith. Berdyaev has a philosopher's perspective on the future – but his vision is not as impenetrable as it sounds; his observation that 'true life is creativity, not development: it is the freedom for creative arts, for creative fire, rather than necessity and the heaviness of congealing self-perfection'[3] captures perfectly the distinction between transfiguration and mere change. It's the difference between *creative fire* and *congealing self-perfection.*

Having a proper concern for the processes of the Church and taking proper care over the standards of our worship and interaction is not at issue. But we might all recognise the *congealing self-perfection* that comes from an over-emphasis on self-justification rather than a reliance on the transfiguring power of God.

One of our tasks as Christian people in the world is to seek out those experiences and places where transfiguration is made possible. We can live our lives open to the prospect of ennobling and dignifying experiences. And if Berdyaev is right, it is in our creativity we'll find those places.

Liturgy is one of those potentially transfiguring mountaintop places; when the creative energy of the music lifts our spirits beyond the walls of a beautiful church to see the agony and ecstasy of the world as it really is. When the attempt to communicate with God in words and music and in the very walls of the building seems to be taking every ounce of energy that we have. When we realise that the building itself is a prayer; it is itself an attempt to reach God, to evoke heaven; to join in the songs of the angels, when a song is sung by a community rooted in its desire to offer prayers to God.

Silence is potentially a transfiguring experience; when the depths of ourselves are plumbed; when we dare to spend time alone without distraction, where we let God hear the tinnitus of fears and confusions that deafen us in our everyday interactions. Where we take off the mask we wear in front of others and let God see the light and fire that is deep within us.

Love is potentially a transfiguring experience; when we know ourselves to be beautiful in another's eyes; when a friend is spectacularly kind; when a lover touches us with tenderness; when our family accepts us as we are.

The natural world too can be transfiguring for us; when the mountaintop seems worth the climb; when the ocean's depths reveal the abundance of life and variety of colour and form; when the sun is bright or the wind is strong, or the vivid sky compels us to look up.

We will all have our own thoughts; but the point is we are invited through our own imaginations and innate creativity to join the transfiguring power of God in the world. Jesus Christ was supremely open to this creativity and, even from the cross, was creating new communities, new relationships, in two people who were gazing together at the worst catastrophe they had ever seen.

Suffering and glory are our meditation. God in Jesus Christ turns us to one another as we steady our gaze on the tragedy of the world.

The second concern we identified as a difficulty for church communities is the sometimes earthbound nature of church culture. Let's explore what Jesus' word to Mary and John teaches us about this.

We may feel slightly diffident towards or even unsettled by this word from the cross to them. For Mary the mother of Jesus, and John the beloved disciple, may well have both been focused entirely on Jesus with love. Whatever their thoughts, and even if they reached sideways in a gesture of physical comfort one to another, their attention was wrapped up in Jesus and their relationship and response to him – and their desire for a response from him. Perhaps when Mary saw he was to speak again she hoped in their heart that he would speak to *her*, and validate her love. John, the same.

Instead, these words turned the gaze away from him to one another. *Woman, behold your son*. Her eyes did not want to follow Jesus' words to the face of one beside her. He was not the one she loved, had birthed, held and helped. *Behold your mother*. John's response to the words was as one who loved and followed Jesus, and he was being given the privilege of doing work his teacher could no longer do. John's enthusiasm for Mary was derivative. Perhaps.

Jesus' word to Mary and John is to behold one another; and to us, to behold our brother and sister beside us; to behold. '*Ide,*' says Jesus; 'Look!'

As we approach the cross this command turns us to each other; to look, to see the other as they are; to *behold* another and to look with compassion.

Jesus beheld Bartimaeus, and the man with the withered hand, and the woman caught in adultery – before their transfiguring encounters with him. And now he asks Mary and John to behold one another in a new way. Their faces, disfigured by grief, could be transfigured by love.

The poet writes:

> Yes, yours, my love, is the right human face.
> I in my mind had waited for this long,
> Seeing the false and searching for the true,
> Then found you as a traveller finds a place
> Of welcome suddenly amid the wrong
> Valleys and rocks and twisting roads.[4]

This inspires but it still leaves us with our problem about the challenge of church culture.

If Jesus was creating a new family, not tied to ethnicity, hereditary considerations, even shared background or interest, then what are the characteristics of that family, those new relationships? What kind of new community did Jesus create?

First, these new relationships are contemplative. Jesus asks us from the cross to behold one another. To behold implies a stillness, a contemplation of the other that by its daring acceptance of another delegitimises the structures of dominance and verbal violence that often characterise our work or personal relationships. To behold another speaks of mutuality, a refusal to give in to the impulse for a moment of ridicule or attack of another that is designed to make us feel more secure. To behold is to value the story in another's face, and to respect the difference from our own.

Second, these new relationships are creative. Church communities can challenge the fault lines that in society keep us apart: of generation, class, ethnicity, economic circumstances. In increasingly individualistic days too, the church is a place where face-to-face relationships foster authenticity and lead us in our relationships with one another from well-intentioned sincerity to a more vital and stretching truth. We have a choice, particularly in our cities: whether to withdraw to our laptops and communicate with thousands of people without ever seeing them, or whether to continue to gather, to meet to worship God and to care for each other.

To return to our theme of transfiguration: 'Christianity does not ask us to live in the shadow of the cross but in the fire of its creative action.'[5]

Third, these new relationships endure. It's seductive for us to make choices about our relationships based primarily or even entirely on what good this might do me; what I might get out of it. The relationship between Mary and John that Jesus inaugurates from the cross is mutual and enduring and primarily about the other. Of course we receive benefit from our engagement with each other; but there is a kind of 'despite everything' type of faith in each other that we are called to live.

Fourth, these new relationships are sacramental, based not around a Sunday liturgical club but a pattern of association that is sacramental in the everyday, a breaking in of eternity into time as we behold one another. In the poet's words, we see the *right* human face – in *every* human face. This commitment will bring us sorrow, serenity, connection and truth.

Even from the place of terrible suffering that Jesus speaks this word, he is urging us to new possibilities. In this word, we are told that God does not weary as we do of our pettiness and our selfishness, God does not weary as we do of the desire to keep travelling together. Real life is now with the people God has given us to love. In this is authenticity and truth.

A Brazilian poet wrote compellingly of Jesus, 'He is as beautiful as a Yes/ in a room full of Nos.'[6]

Even broken on the cross Jesus Christ is 'yes': yes to contemplation, transfiguration, creation and community; yes to hope and to the best days – which are yet to come.

> Woman, behold your Son; Yes.
> Behold your mother: Yes.
>
> *He is as beautiful as a Yes*
> *in a room full of Nos.*
> *He is as beautiful as the second harvest*
> *that increases the sugar cane field's yield.*
> *Beautiful because he is a door*
> *that turns into many exits.*
> *Beautiful like the final wave*
> *that no seashore devours.*
> *He is as beautiful as the waves*
> *in the sum of their infinity.*

Music: Track 4 'Behold Your Son, Behold Your Mother'

'Eli, Eli, lama sabachthani?
... My God, my God, why hast
thou forsaken me?'

(Matthew 27:46)

TARJEI PARK

The scene could hardly have been more different from Calvary. It was a crystal clear September morning in New York, the start of the working day. And something happened, something that was to horrify a planet. At 8.46 a.m. a Boeing 767 passenger airliner was flown into the north tower of the World Trade Center. Fifteen minutes later America and the world watched live news footage of a second 767 flying directly into the south tower. It was a moment simultaneously horrifying and unbelievable. As this second plane ploughed into the tower 10,000 gallons of fuel exploded in a fireball against and within the building. Two more planes would fall and people would die. Millions watched the images with tears in their eyes as they were televised and re-televised. Even in the days following it was impossible for many to look at the newspaper photographs of bodies falling from the towers without wanting to weep.

Weeping at heartbreaking images has become an all too familiar experience in these opening years of the twenty-first century. Just as those haunting images of the attacks on the World Trade Center will be remembered for a very long time, so too will the video footage taken by tourists on beaches off the Indian Ocean on 26 December 2004. Early that day, as millions of people were going about their morning business, and thousands of tourists were relaxing on beaches, a tsunami struck that devastated coastal areas in the region. The video footage is a poignant reminder of the tragedy. Curious tourists spotted the unusual wave and captured its approach on camera, totally unaware of its size, speed or power – until it was too late. The impact of the tidal wave and subsequent flooding claimed the lives of nearly 300,000 people. Around 100,000 people went missing, presumed dead. Over 5 million people became homeless, hungry and exposed to the risk of disease.

Similarly, video images captured on mobile phones by travellers escaping from the wrecked carriages of underground trains in London on 7 July 2005 will long live in people's memory. The dark and grainy pictures are a haunting reminder of the first suicide bombings in Britain, and of the needless loss of life and the physical and mental injuries inflicted upon those who happened to be travelling at that time.

In the days that followed these tragic events, and again following the devastation wrought by Hurricane Katrina in the United States in late August 2005, there were many gestures and acts of solidarity across the world for their innocent victims. Places of worship were filled to overflowing as mourners lamented and prayed to God. But others despaired of God. As the world tried to make sense of the Indian Ocean tsunami, the worst natural disaster in living memory, thoughts turned back to a similar event on Sunday 1 November 1775, when a tidal wave struck the coastline of Portugal and Spain. After what became known as the Lisbon earthquake, serious questions of faith were raised across Christian Europe. How could a loving God allow the suffering of innocent victims? How could God abandon humanity in this way? For some, their faith was shattered. Others cried out '*Why?*'

Why not despair of God? Why not believe that God is somehow answerable? Why not cry out 'Why?' Did Jesus not do this on the cross, and in so doing echo the self-same cry of dereliction made by millions of others across the ages, 'My God, my God, why hast thou forsaken me?'

There is no emotionally satisfactory answer to these questions when they are asked by people in despair. Talk of God's non-intervention as being part of the gift of free will is of little consolation, and seems to go against a good many passages from Scripture. There are times when the blunt cruelty of a situation is tested beyond any casual theological speculation. This is movingly conveyed in David Scott's poem 'Dean Tait'. Archibald Tait was Dean of Carlisle, and later Archbishop of Canterbury, and in the space of one month, March 1856, five of his daughters died in an epidemic of scarlet fever.

> Quite put aside were any thoughts
> of the state of the Cathedral roof.
> Instead a quiet agony, waiting
> for the stethoscope's final figure of eight,
> and the click of the doctor's bag.
> He never thought there could be this routine
> to death: the prayer book, the size of his palm;
> his wife, half in doubt because of the fever,
> hiding the sick-room drawings away;
> and at their prayers each day
> in a borrowed house, they tested
> the Bible texts against a silent nursery.[1]

Where is God in all this? What responsibility does God have for it? When appalling cruelty, suffering and evil occur these are not idle questions, they are natural questions made by the faithful to their God. The answer to these questions is not necessarily a comfortable one. And conclusions reached can challenge our whole view of who God is.

Elie Wiesel recalls a hauntingly painful event that he experienced as a teenager in Auschwitz. A teacher of Talmud who had befriended Wiesel in the Nazi death camp took him one night back to his own barracks where three erudite rabbis decided to put God on trial. They decided in 'a rabbinic court of law to indict the Almighty' for 'allowing His children to be massacred'. Over several nights, evidence was presented and then a unanimous verdict was reached: 'the Lord God Almighty, Creator of Heaven and Earth, was found *guilty* of crimes against creation and humankind.' Wiesel writes, 'I remember: I was there, and I felt like crying. But there nobody cried.' Then, after an 'infinity of silence', one of them looked at the sky and said, 'It's time for evening prayers', and they all recited Maariv, the evening service.[2]

There can be no obvious response to this trial and to the prayerful sequel. Powerful ambiguity remains. The God they prayed to *had* been found guilty – guilty of not intervening to halt great evil – not only in Auschwitz but also in Rwanda, in New York, in London, New Orleans, across the Indian Ocean, in the prisons and in the famines and in the quiet spread of AIDS across the earth.

Even if God does not intervene, can God abandon one – for is not God *present* everywhere, as Psalm 139 beautifully evokes?

> Where can I go from your spirit?
> Or where can I flee from your presence?
> If I ascend to heaven, you are there;
> if I make my bed in Sheol, you are there.
> If I take the wings of the morning
> and settle at the farthest limits of the sea,
> even there your hand shall lead me,
> and your right hand shall hold me fast.
> (Ps. 139:7–10)

The realisation that God is present even when God does not *intervene* is not a loss of belief in God. It is the recognition of who God is and who we are. We are inextricably united to God, but in ways we often cannot detect.

This is the heart of mature spirituality: to affirm God even when God's hiddenness is at its most real. Inscribed on a cellar wall in Cologne where some Jews had hidden for the entire duration of the Second World War were these lines:

> I believe in the sun, even when it doesn't shine.
> I believe in love, even when I don't feel it.
> I believe in God, even when He is silent.

The concept of the hiddenness of God is profoundly scriptural. In Isaiah we read, 'Truly, you are a God who hides himself, O God of Israel, the Saviour' (45:15). The sixteenth-century spiritual teacher John of the Cross likewise began one of his famous poems by crying out to God not in desperation but in searching faith, 'Where have you hidden, beloved?' And in Christian theology the notion of the 'hidden God' assures that God is not completely domesticated by psychological needs. There is always that of God which transcends human understanding; that of God which is beyond our sight.

So where do we go from here? Where does Christ's cry of dereliction from the cross leave us? Or, rather, where does it take us? It takes us to a bleak place, a place of absence. It takes us to a place where Jesus has been, where he cried out, 'My God, my God, why hast thou forsaken me?' But the dereliction on the cross is not the end of the story.

Jesus Christ suffered as a human being, and that human experience is taken up into divinity – *crucified* humanity is taken up into divinity.

There is no evil which can separate us from Jesus Christ, and so there is no evil that can separate us from God. For Jesus was not abandoned ultimately. No, that dark and desolate Friday afternoon is not the end of the story, because through Jesus Christ's risen and ascended crucified brokenness God searches out the broken of this world with the hope of new life. Among the tools God uses to search through the world are God's people. They are you and me. They are the fire-fighters in New York City who courageously ran through a twenty-first-century vision of hell to help others. They are the people who stretched out their hands amid the terror to grab children being washed out to sea. They are the Jews in Cologne who left behind for us their insights of faith. In our suffering, God 'intervenes' through the broken and healed humanity of Christ. There is something of the divine will in this saving work, and it speaks not of abandonment but of solidarity with humanity in hell.

> *Oh, where have you been, my blue-eyed son?*
> *Oh, where have you been, my darling one?*
> *I met a young woman whose body was burning*
> *and it's a hard rain's a-gonna fall.*[3]

Hell on earth is a reality. There are occasions in life that are so crushingly evil. There are sights seen that just should not be seen. There are extremes of cruelty that are just not acceptable. There are times of such sadness that they break your heart. There are places we just should not have to be.

Why?

He 'was crucified, dead, and buried: He descended into hell.'

What was Jesus doing in hell? He was looking for his friend Judas Iscariot. Judas had done something so wrong he could not forgive himself, and feeling incapable of being forgiven, in bitter tears of regret, he hanged himself. Well, Jesus went looking for him, and in hell he found him. He walked over to him, kissed him, and took his hand.

Miracles occur in hell.

When we see images on the television or in magazines and books it is often evil visited on children that makes us cry: the dehydrated child in Nepal with flies on her cheeks, the terrified boy in Gaza tucked up against his father crying before he is shot, the wide-eyed AIDS orphan wandering the countryside in Botswana. And these really are moments of hell on earth.

Loveliness happens too.

There was a brother and sister on the television news, he was about

eight and she was about four, they had become separated from their family following the dreadful flooding in Mozambique in the spring of 2000;
their family might not even be alive. They had managed to get a bag of
maize meal from one of the relief camps, but they were not going to open
it – it was to be a present for their parents when they found them. After
talking to the news correspondent they ran off together to continue the
search for their family. The boy was so caring of his sister. The love and
responsibility of these two poor children was just heart-achingly beautiful.

> Jésus le Christ, lumière intérieure,
> ne laisse pas mes ténèbres me parler.
> Jésus le Christ, lumière intérieure,
> donne-moi d'accueillir ton amour.
>
> Lord Jesus Christ, your light shines within us.
> Let not my doubts nor my darkness speak to me.
> Lord Jesus Christ, your light shines within us.
> Let my heart always welcome your love.[4]

Music: Track 5 'Credo'

'I thirst' (John 19:28)

SABINA ALKIRE

'Our charism is to satiate the thirst of Jesus for love and souls – by working at the salvation and sanctification of the poorest of the poor.'[1] Responding to this last word of Christ is the public purpose of Mother Teresa's sisters and brothers, the heart of the calling to serve the poor she received on her train journey to Darjeeling, and the spiritual focus of her community now that she is gone. Every convent chapel of the Missionaries of Charity throughout the world, whether active or contemplative, has a bloody crucifix and by it – always – two words: 'I thirst.' They are generally pasted up in paper letters, which arc slightly away from the wall at the tips. And most visitors come and go without noticing the saying. If they glimpse it at all, they rarely grasp its significance.

But the phrase is highly significant. The fifth last word – 'I am thirsting' (in the present continuous tense) – represents to this community an insight that gives a sure-footed joy to their work, an insight that deserves to be shared, although without the usual romance with which journalists paint these sisters in blue-rimmed saris.

The insight is that the thirst of Christ on the cross and the thirst of Christ in the living poor are one and the same. Towards the end of Matthew's gospel Jesus tells a story of judgement, where the Son of Man separates the sheep from the goats, and the chosen query:

'Lord, when was it that we saw you hungry and gave you food, or thirsty and gave you drink? And when was it that we saw you a stranger and welcomed you or naked and gave you clothing? And when was it that we saw you sick or in prison and visited you?' (25:37–39)

Here, too, is an image of a thirsting Lord.

The image of a thirsting Lord leads to a different way of hearing the word of Christ on the cross. Sometimes when we ponder the words 'I thirst', we consider the painful dehydration of a body that had been up to 18 hours without water, that had lost blood through the scourging by leather laced with bone shards and the crown of thorns, and is now hung in the sun. So we realise with a start that in these alone of the seven last words Jesus spoke of himself – his own physical agony – which we may not have realised so acutely before. We begin to grasp that Jesus suffered. Sometimes when we ponder 'I thirst' we realise how central this utterance, this lone expression of bodily need, was to the doctrinal jigsaw puzzle the early Church tried to assemble: how did the fragile human body of the person of Jesus fit together with his divinity? And so we probe the mystery of the incarnation – of God made flesh.

However we appreciate this utterance, whether through sharpened imagination or through a historical entrée into the controversies of the early Church, we tend to consider it in the past. In contrast, Mother Teresa's sisters and brothers hear the words in the present. They hear 'I thirst' in the stumpy limbs of the leper, in the slumped shoulders of the depressed and unloved, in the watchful eyes of the AIDS patient, the lilting voice of the orphan, and the rasp of the dying. The insight, the recognition that gives rise to action, is that these words are true for God in the present. Christ is present in those that suffer. 'Jesus makes Himself the hungry one, the naked one, the homeless one, the unwanted one, and He says, "[just as you did it to one of the least of these who are members of my family] You did it to Me."'[2] As Mother Teresa put it in a letter to her community, '"I Thirst" and "You did it to me" – Remember always to connect the two."[3]

But who are 'the least of these'? It is hard for those of us who perch at one point on a planet overloaded with information to take in what is going on around us. Perhaps we might consider a series of 'aerial photos', if you will, of the human family.

Our planet houses just over six billion people. Of these, one billion of us live on less than $1 a day. One in seven of us are malnourished.[4] One in six of us do not have clean water to drink. Well over one in three of us do not have basic sanitation. Nearly half of us live on less than $2 a day. If we asked the population of the world to sit down in representative groups of four people, three out of the four members of each group would be from a developing country. If we were then to feed ourselves, the three people from developing countries would get one piece of toast each, while the person from the developed country would get seven pieces of toast – every day, every meal. If there were sixty technological gadgets to distribute, the three developing country group members would get one each; the fourth person would collect the remaining fifty-seven. If we converted all energy units into batteries, the three persons would use one battery each; the fourth person would use up seventeen batteries in the same time period.[5] We could go on …

The obvious thing to do in the face of such inequality is to share, and we do – a little. If the wealthy person of the group had $1000 and was from the USA, he or she would give the other three $1.60 in total 'foreign aid'; if the person were British it would be $3.60. If the person were Norwegian it would be $8.70. No representative person on the planet gives more.[6] On average throughout all of the groups, the three developing country members would get $2.50 between them in foreign aid, and the fourth member would retain $997.50, out of which he or she would give another 30 cents as a private donation, retaining $997.20.

One final number is necessary. About one in three persons on the globe self-identifies their religious affiliation as Christian. *That is two billion people!* These are people who walk the corridors of power and people who live on the margins of society and people in all walks of life in between. Not all of us are destitute. The faith has been around, and the Church has been active throughout the evolutions that created this profile of poverty and wealth. Christianity is the dominant religious affiliation among the people with seven pieces of toast and fifty-seven gadgets and seventeen used-up batteries on their laps. And yet there is so much poverty. Gandhi is often cited as saying, 'If Christians lived out their faith fully there would be no Hindus left in India.' It might not be terribly awry to muse that 'If Christians had lived out their faith fully there would not be such poverty on earth.'

How do Christians live out the faith? How do we apply the same energetic love and spiritual depth that Mother Teresa's sisters show, to such a litany of poverties?

Clearly, addressing 'the least of these my brothers and sisters' requires urgent responses for immediate needs: of the aged, the ill, the addicts, the orphaned, those with AIDS. But responding to urgent needs alone is not and will never be enough. Structural change, too, is required: in trade, aid and debt relief, but also in business, communications and entertainment; in research and teaching and foreign policy. As the American civil rights activist Martin Luther King Jr wrote:

> [W]e are called to play the good Samaritan on life's roadside; but that will be only an initial act. One day we must come to see that the whole Jericho road must be transformed so that men and women will not be constantly beaten and robbed as they make their journey on life's highway. True compassion is more than flinging a coin to a beggar; it is not haphazard and superficial. It comes to see that an edifice which produces beggars needs restructuring.[7]

But somehow, a tightly reasoned argument against intellectual property rights or trade regimes does not seem to evoke the same compassion as a skeletal figure on a distant street corner. The daily routine of memos and speeches, of staff meetings and scantily skimmed reports is a far cry from the daily rhythm of washing clothes, bathing, feeding, playing with and befriending the poor. The privilege of meeting Christ in the 'distressing disguise of the poor' – which can itself be a religious experience – simply may not occur. Those who work for justice – for changes of policy or structure – may be thrice removed from the faces of those they serve, and may not know the results of their actions (for good or ill). And so often their actions seem tainted with compromise: pushy, naive or far-fetched. So beyond these actions, again we ask, how do we live out our faith?

It would be tempting – almost natural – to try to address structures of injustice armed with facts and considerations alone, striking out in anger or hope, yet leaving off the roots of prayer and of Christian community. Yet what would it be to be a 'contemplative in the heart of the world' while working for structural change? What would it be to attend to the thirst of Christ in the legislative assemblies or research institutes or executive offices?

It would be to stand still, once in a while, centre, and listen. Dag Hammerskjöld, the visionary leader of the United Nations, tried to root his professional work in this stillness. He wrote, 'How can you expect to keep your powers of hearing when you never want to listen? That God should have time for you, you seem to take as much for granted as that you cannot have time for Him.'[8] Even the World Bank has, within a second basement's fluorescent cubicles, an inauspicious meditation room containing miscellaneous prayer carpets and donated artwork. Staff can retreat, take off their shoes and be still.

We can also seek out our God in unlikely professional environs. John of the Cross, a Spanish mystic and poet, suggested that we approach God *anywhere* with a particular combination of utter awe and persistent curiosity. He wrote:

> You honour God greatly and indeed come near to him, when you hold [God] to be nobler and deeper than anything you can attain. So ... do not be like many heartless people who

have a low opinion of God: they think that when they cannot understand him or sense or feel him, he is further away – when the truth is more the opposite: it is when you understand [God] less clearly that you are coming closer ... So you do well at all times, whether life, or faith, is smooth, or hard, you do well to hold God as hidden, and so to cry out to him, 'Where have you hidden?'[9]

We live out our faith by depending on our faith. And faith becomes stronger the more we ask of God, 'Where have you hidden?'

The thirst of Christ and the aching wounds of the poor demand a response. And God is present to guide our response; indeed God yearns to do so – even in unlikely professional environs. Seeking out God even if we do not feel God grounds our action in listening, contemplation and a wisdom wider than our own. And by this ground we respond to the thirst of God, as well as to those who thirst among us. For, in words attributed to the mystic, intellectual and energetic spiritual Mother of the Carmelite renewal, St Teresa of Avila, 'Christ has no body now but yours; no hands, no feet on earth but yours; yours are the eyes through which he looks salvation on the world.'

Can you – can we – can the Church – without self-importance or aggrandisement – bear our mundane part in addressing Jesus' thirst as it comes to us today? Can we do it not only as churchgoers but also as professionals, citizens, parents and volunteers? Please God may it be our joy and our burden to do so.

Music: Track 6 'They Shall Be Comforted'

'It is finished' (John 19:30)

SABINA ALKIRE

'It is finished,' Jesus says from the cross. *Tetelestai* is the Greek. Things have reached their *telos:* their conclusion, and also their goal. It is fulfilled. It has been accomplished.[1]

What an extraordinary thing for a 33-year-old person to say! Jesus was just coming into his prime: teaching people the ways of love, healing people from illness, caring for the marginalised, developing a movement and new leaders. Maybe he would eventually free the Jewish people from their Roman oppressors. Instead, his life is cut short by a brutal regime. From our perspective this seems a tragedy, but he spoke of fulfilment. Why?

The answer surely lies in a conviction that permeates John's gospel: that Christ's vocation was to do the will of his Father and to accomplish his work. And somehow, he had done what he was meant to do.

It is good to rest with these words of Christ on the cross, for we live in a world where religious groups are still persecuted, where violence is still glorified, where disasters still terrorise, where people still struggle to find community, where Lazarus still sits in hunger at the gate of the rich man. So much of what we understand the will of God to be remains unfinished; unfulfilled.

The scope and depth of these and other problems can seem overwhelming, and beyond our ability to solve. We are tempted by

'Father, into thy hands I commit my spirit!' (Luke 23:46)

LUCY WINKETT

The last word that makes sense of all the rest.

It is the end of a long conversation between Jesus and his Father: this commending, this ending has a context and a history. Jesus commends his spirit not easily or even readily, but at the end of a terrifying struggle in physical pain and spiritual distress.

It echoes the opening words of this, his last conversation, in the garden of Gethsemane 'not my will but yours'. The conversation that started with resolve and ends with surrender.

He is pinned, so close to death. He is dis-abled; unable to move. Rigid with the approach of the end. At that – hopeless – moment he does the most hopeful thing; and gives himself into the hands of God.

It's nearly over and we look together as believers at the broken body of God.

The poet writes:

> Deliver me from the long drought
>   of the mind. Let leaves
> from the deciduous Cross
>   fall on us, washing
> us clean, turning our autumn
>   to gold by the affluence of their fountain.[1]

We stand now on the boundary between life and death; the moment of travel is upon us and we know we will take the first step with him. We are looking together beyond ourselves – into the unknown – into the place where we commend our spirits. And while we gaze at this broken body on the cross, we know – although we wish we didn't – that Christ's body broken on earth today is the Church. Perhaps it has to be that when we have torn each other apart we will say, *into your hands* – at the end of a conversation that began with resolve and will end in surrender.

As the worldwide Church we are the broken body of Christ. We grieve for a unity that seems to be beyond our imaginations. It seems that schism is one of the certainties of Christian history; at different times and for different reasons and with different people leading the way. But separation is a last resort. We want to stay whole.

Historically, there are two strands of Christian theology which it seems are pertinent in these uncertain days for the Anglican Communion. In 434 the monk/theologian Vincent of Lerins articulated the basis of the Catholic understanding of the nature of the Church: 'In the Catholic Church ... all possible care must be taken that we hold that faith which has been believed everywhere, always, by all.'[2]

This threefold test of Catholicity from the fifth century – *everywhere, always, by all* – was a benchmark, against which to test true and false developments in tradition and practice, and it was a means of identifying those who failed the test.

It was always surely a fantasy – that all Christians would hold the same universal, timeless version of faith. Christianity by its very nature is a historical faith. We take history seriously and we give a voice to those who are long dead. As we do so, we affirm our belief in the resurrection and we affirm our belief in the communion of saints. But it also increases the number of voices that we hear, the number of interpretations of our four gospels, and it makes a living faith relevant and supple, more not less necessary. The fantasy of an identifiable and containable faith, believed everywhere, always, by all is strong and seductive, and by wanting it we reveal our yearning for a simpler, more straightforward life where we don't have to deal with our differences. Ever since Barnabas and Paul sailed away from each other after their argument over John Mark, the Church has had to deal with strong differences of opinion. *Everywhere, always, by all* is a model of church that may be achievable in an agrarian and stable society; but we are in a globalised urban context now. This kind of theology fell asleep in the village and is struggling with the waking nightmare of the city.

It is hard for us to accept that we might believe differently now from the first disciples. Here, as Jesus commends his spirit into the hands of God, his friends are nowhere to be seen. They had simply left their nets, their jobs, their families and followed him for three years. Now it was over, they were hurt, frightened, in hiding. The simple and compelling 'Follow me' had led to this execution and they couldn't stay. Not for this.

We too are called to follow Jesus to the cross, but to follow knowing the ending of this story. We follow a saviour who is already crucified, already risen and present now in the world today. So we see the world in that pattern: life, death, life. It makes sense of the world for us. But we live in the knowledge that many people have believed differently from us in the past, and in the present live their lives on earth following Jesus differently from us, or with entirely different world views. We cannot live grieving for a past that hardly existed; when the same simple faith was held everywhere, always, by all. Unity takes account of the voices across continents and centuries.

The second strand of theology concerns the nature of Jesus as the victim on the cross. When we seek to follow Jesus to the cross and beyond, we are limited by our own, necessarily partial, interpretation of the sacrifice. If Jesus was the victim in the sacrifice, we are surely to be very careful about how we follow his particular path.

What do we have to do? Surrender? Commend our spirits? To God, yes; but to each other?

How do we understand the sacrifice of Jesus and how do we follow him as disciples? What might our calling be within our understanding of Jesus as the ultimate victim? We can translate this, if we are not careful, as a dug-in passive aggression: the more we are told we are wrong the more we know ourselves to be right. In reality, the world is not so neatly divided as we might imagine into goodies and baddies, oppressors and victims. Victims can end up being blamed or blaming themselves and the juxtaposition of victimhood and judgement is a treacherous one.

As Rowan Williams has argued, only the absolute victim can be the merciful, vindicating judge.[3] Jesus on the cross embodies the condition of a pure victim. He accepts – he does not condemn, resist or exclude. His life embodies an unconditional, universal acceptance of people (in a context of social, ritual and racial exclusiveness) and now, he embodies acceptance of his story with this ending. 'Jesus can be the judge because he is victim and the very fact that he is victim means he is a judge who will not condemn.'[4]

Our role is different: we are urged not to judge one another but to love one another. Because of our insecurity and hurt, because we sometimes speak to each other out of our fantasy, we can hurt one another in institutional violence of a lacerating kind.

A nineteenth-century Bishop of London, Mandell Creighton, was deeply frustrated with the Church of England's tendency to divide and condemn. His words written in 1899 have a contemporary resonance: 'It is a cheap line to denounce,' he wrote, 'it satisfies the sense that something ought to be done. I am weary of denunciation.'

The body of the Church is broken by the nails of our own denunciations and judgements, splitting apart the hands that might receive the spirit of another. We are all capable of abusive behaviour, cashing out our theology to increase our own power and justify ourselves. It takes courage for any of us to admit that we could be wrong, but in doing so, we start to turn our faces away from the one with whom we are arguing and towards the mystery of the living God. To speak about strongly held beliefs and feelings is part of how we engage with each other as Christians. We are a Church that wants to try to articulate, to speak, to utter.

The Palestinian Quaker leader and writer Jean Zaru has said that to cry out is to open a dialogue with the oppressor. It is important to cry out, to cry to God. To say something is as important as it is to be silent. That Jesus spoke at all to his Father from the cross is a teaching for us who stand watching. The Eternal Word cried out to the Creator at a moment in time. To speak – to God and to each other – about the condition we find ourselves in is fundamental, fulfilling our need to communicate who and how we are. 'Before we can surrender ourselves we must become ourselves. No one can give up what they do not possess,' said Thomas Merton.

Jesus lived a radically challenging way of love and justice – healing, feeding, liberating, eating with sinners. But at the end he was pinned, bound … confined. Silent.

And so perhaps similarly we are confined; for it may be that we are in a place where words do not help anymore. This place is difficult for such a wordy church – but the process of de-articulation is an important one. We are driven into silence.

We do not agree about the authority of women in ordained ministry. We do not agree about the rightness or wrongness of same-sex relationships. We have elevated these issues almost above all others in our anxiety over the fact that we simply *do not agree.*

It is a cliché to say that we need to listen twice as much as we speak, but like most clichés, it is true. Our arguments are often joyless and have become cruel. We find that we wish to discourage and even kill the fragile faith of those with whom we disagree. We sit around a table – even a communion table – secretly believing we are right. People leave the church because of the intensity of our introspection and we lose perspective.

We will not argue ourselves into communion; and more importantly in the Church of England, we will not legislate our way to unity. In all our divided and contradictory positions, the last thing that we should abandon is our sharing of the bread and wine, the body and the blood. It is often the first.

What do we do about this? One thing we could do is to understand that there is a time for silence, and that we leave off argument, and turn to other parts of God's mission. In the words of Sheila Cassidy, the Church is called to find those people who are poor in our own communities and 'somehow become involved in washing their feet'.[5] In a spirit of realistic ecumenism, we can do what we can together and put to one side those things that in this life keep us apart. It is only the mission of the Church that can unite us. We are to be in 'conversation mode' with the institutions and peoples with whom we are surrounded, listening, sharing our faith and our experience of life in the world.[6] More importantly than the talking will be the doing, finding practical ways to witness to Christ's presence in the world together. After a while when we've been working together for love of all those people who do not belong, we will look up one day and find ourselves alongside each other – and realise that while we may still not agree, we've moved on.

Most of all we could focus not on our own anxiety but on the one who is beyond all of us. What binds us is a combined gazing at the mystery of Christ – his life, his death, his ongoing presence among us.

The eternal conversation of which we are part, between God and humanity, continues on in Christ's name and after his example: the suffering peoples of God will cry out in this way to their Creator as human lives are broken and love is crucified again.

This last word of commendation is a moment of gift and commitment to the One who is beyond all words. The broken Church will similarly continue to cry out, perhaps only in the last resort, in the moment before death, as we try to commend ourselves together to our Creator. Unity (based on uniformity) is not our God, and cannot become our idol. We are broken and will break apart again; but when we do, we break trusting that in God what is irreconcilable on earth is somehow redeemed, reconciled and raised to new life in heaven.

Music: Track 8 'The Surrender'

At the ninth hour

It is the ninth hour. We have waited. And listened. And have watched him die. We are tired but relieved that the suffering is over. Our world has changed. The world has changed.

Let us pray.

Lord, we have witnessed your suffering and heard your words.
Give us strength to follow in your resurrection life.
And as we leave this place, may we live these words in the world you came to save.
Amen. ·

Notes

Seven last words from the cross (Richard Harries)

1. John Wilkinson, *Egeria's Travels* (Warminster, Aris & Phillips, 1999), pp. 75–7, 154–7.
2. Herbert Thurston, *Lent and Holy Week* (London, 1906), pp. 383–4.
3. Ibid. p. 386.
4. Alonso Messia (trans. with an introduction by Herbert Thurston), *The Devotion of the Three Hours' Agony on Good Friday* (London, Sands and Co., 1899), p. 4.
5. From a broadcast on BBC Radio 4, 31 July 1981.

The cross in the 21st century (Rowan Williams)

1. Charles Causley, *Collected Poems 1951–1975* (London, Macmillan, 1975), p. 69.

'Father, forgive them; for they know not what they do' (Edmund Newell)

1. Friedrich Heer, *God's First Love: Christians and Jews over Two Thousand Years* (London, Weidenfeld and Nicholson, 1999), pp. 36–7.
2. St Chrysostom, *Sixth Oration Against the Jews*.
3. Quoted in Charlotte Klein, *Anti Judaism in Christian Theology* (London, SPCK, 1978), p. 118.
4. James Shapiro, *Oberammergau: The Troubling Story of the World's Most Famous Passion Play* (London, Little, Brown, 2000), p. 28.

'Truly, I say to you, today you will be with me in Paradise (Giles Fraser)

1. Brian Cheyette, review of *Schindler's List, Times Literary Supplement*, 18 February 1994.

2. Mary Midgely, *Wickedness: A Philosophical Essay* (London, Routledge, 1984), p. 114.
3. Ibid. p. 115.
4. Gillian Rose, *Mourning Becomes the Law: Philosophy and Representation* (Cambridge University Press, 1996), p. 45.
5. Christopher Browning, *Ordinary Men: Reserve Police Battalion 101 and the Final Solution in Poland* (New York, HarperCollins, 1992).

'Woman, behold your son! . . . Behold your mother!' (Lucy Winkett)

1. Richard Harries, *God Outside the Box: Why Spiritual People Object to Christianity* (London, SPCK, 2002), p. ix.
2. Dorothee Soelle, *The Silent Cry: Mysticism and Resistance* (Minneapolis, MN, Fortress Press, 2001).
3. N. Berdyaev (trans. N. Duddington), *The Destiny of Man*, (London, G. Bles, 1937), p. 140.
4. Edwin Muir, 'The Confirmation', *Collected Poems* (London, Faber and Faber, 1984), p. 118.
5. Pierre Teilhard de Chardin, quoted in John Moses (ed.), *The Desert: An Anthology for Lent*, (Norwich, Canterbury Press, 1997), p. 63.
6. Joao Cabral de Melo Neto, *Tod und Leben des Severino*, (St Gallen and Wapertal, 1985), p. 85.

'Eli, Eli, lama sabachthani? . . . My God, my God, why hast thou forsaken me?' (Tarjei Park)

1. David Scott, *Selected Poems* (Bloodaxe Books, 1998), p. 47.
2. Elie Wiesel, *The Trial of God* (Shocken, 1995), pp. vii, xxiii.
3. Bob Dylan, 'A Hard Rain's A-Gonna Fall' on *The Freewheelin' Bob Dylan* (CBS, 1963).
4. Ateliers et Presses de Taizé, F-71250 Taizé-Communauté.

'I thirst' (Sabina Alkire)

1. Quoted from the Constitution of the Missionaries of Charity in George Gorraee, *For Love of God: Mother Teresa of Calcutta* (London, T. Shand Alba Publications, 1974).

2. Whatever You Did Unto One of the Least, You Did Unto Me', Mother Teresa MC in Michael Collopy, *Works of Love are Works of Peace* (Ignatius Press, 1996), pp. 191–6.
3. Ibid.
4. *The State of Food Insecurity in the World 2004*. Food and Agriculture Organization of the United Nations. Rome, Italy. (852 million)
5. Adapted from CAFOD 2001.
6. Preliminary 2004 data.
    http://www.oecd.org/dac
7. 'A Time to Break Silence', address to clergy and laity given at Riverside Church, New York, 4 April 1967, reprinted in James M. Washington (ed.), *A Testament of Hope: The Essential Writings and Speeches of Martin Luther King, Jr* (Harper Collins, San Francisco, 1991) p. 241.
8. Statement by Dag Hammarskjöld, UN Secretary-General (1953–1961) written for the dedication of the United Nations Meditation Room.
9. Quoted and discussed to this effect in Iain Matthews, *Impact of God* (London, Hodder & Stoughton, 1995), p. 97. This is from John's *Canticle* (second redaction) 1.12 see 1.4.

'It is finished' (Sabina Alkire)
1. This opening is based on the opening of Hugh White 'It is finished' in Edmund Newell (ed.), *Seven Words for the 21st Century*, (London, Darton, Longman & Todd, 2002) p. 83.
2. Dag Hammarskjöld, *Markings* (New York, Ballantine Books, 1983), p. 138.
3. Ibid., p. 45.
4. http://www.un.org/Depts/dhl/dag/time1953.htm
5. http://www.un.org/Depts/dhl/dag/time1960.htm
6. Hammarskjöld, *Markings*, p. 71.
7. 'Dag Hammarskjöld: "Virtuoso of Multilateral Diplomacy." – Former UN Secretary-General', *UN Chronicle*, September 1991.
8. http://www.un.org/Depts/dhl/dag/time1958.htm
9. http://www.un.org/Depts/dhl/dag/time1953.htm
10. http://www.nobelprize.org/peace/laureates/1961/hammarskjold-acceptance.html
11. Hammarskjöld, *Markings*, p. 104.

12. Ibid., p. 100.
13. Ibid., p. 83.

'Father, into thy hands I commit my spirit!' (Lucy Winkett)
 1. R. S. Thomas, 'The Prayer', *Collected Poems 1945–1990* (London, Phoenix, 1995), p. 270.
 2. Quoted in *Oxford Dictionary of the Christian Church*, (Oxford University Press, 1997), p. 1700.
 3. Rowan Williams, *Resurrection* (London, Darton, Longman & Todd, 1982), p. 7.
 4. Ibid., p. 8.
 5. Sheila Cassidy, *Good Friday People* (London, Darton, Longman & Todd, 1991).
 6. Duncan J. Dormor, Jeremy Caddick, Jane McDonald (eds), *Anglicanism: The Answer to Modernity* (London, Continuum, 2005).